The Wombat
Who Talked to the Stars

THE JOURNAL OF A NORTHERN HAIRY-NOSED WOMBAT

by Jill Morris
illustrated by Sharon Dye

7000324015527

D0486953

Greater Glider Productions, Maleny, Queensland, Australia

Excellence in Educational Publishing Awards (Primary) 1997
Best Children's Book, Whitley Awards 1997
Shortlisted, Eve Pownall Award 1998
reprinted April 1998, June 1998, (paperback) January 2004

With grateful thanks to
Dr Alan Horsup (Queensland Department of Environment) & members of the Northern Hairy-nosed Wombat Recovery Team; 'The Courier Mail'; the Dennis family; Queensland Museum; Arts Queensland for financial assistance in creative development;

and to
Deryn Alpers, David Blyde, Benn Bryant, Phil Cameron, Patrick Couper, Jeanette Covacevich, Doug Crossman, Murray Evans, Karin Gerhardt, Greg Gordon, Stuart Green, Simon Hoyle, Heather Janetzki, Chris Johnson, Jodie Lardner-Smith, Bill Sherwin, Vernon Steele, Dave Taggart, Andrea Taylor, Peter Temple-Smith, Steve Van Dyck and Andrew Woolnough; and all the other scientists and observers whose work has made it possible for us to share this information with children.

first published 1997 by Greater Glider Productions Australia Pty Ltd
'Book Farm' 8 Rees Lane Maleny 4552 Queensland Australia
edited by Cheryl Wickes & Dr Alan Horsup
typeset by McMillan Type & Design, Melbourne Victoria
printed by Fergies, Hamilton Queensland
bound by Special Equipment, Hemmant Queensland
assembled by Lynne Tracey
designed by Sharon Dye

© text & illustrations
Jill Morris & Sharon Dye 1997

All Rights Reserved. No part of this book may be reproduced, stored in or introduced into a retrieval system, or transmitted, in any form or by any means (electronic, mechanical, photocopying, recording or otherwise), without the prior permission of Greater Glider Productions.

National Library of Australia Cataloguing-in-Publication
Morris, Jill. 1936-,
The wombat who talked to the stars: the journal of a northern hairy-nosed wombat.

Bibliography.
Includes index.
ISBN 0 947304 70 3 (paperback)
ISBN 0 947304 8 2 (hardback)

1. Wombats - Juvenile literature. I. Title.

599.2

WORCESTERSHIRE COUNTY COUNCIL	
152	
Peters	19-Jun-2008
J599.24	£5.99

ARTS QUEENSLAND

Contents

Endangered!

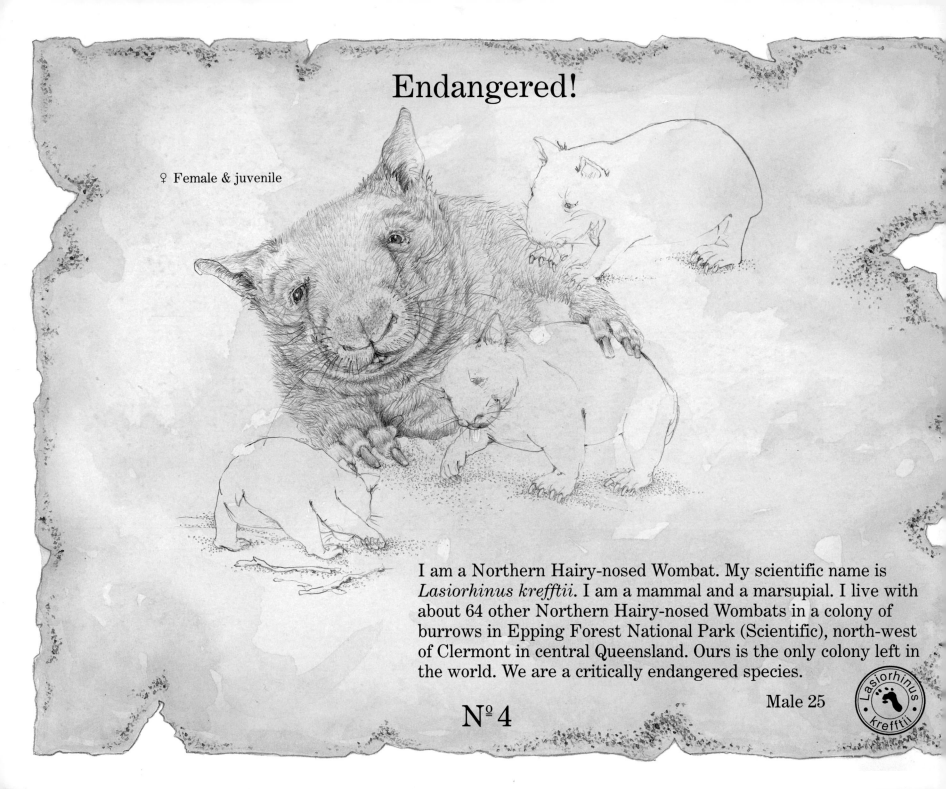

♀ Female & juvenile

I am a Northern Hairy-nosed Wombat. My scientific name is *Lasiorhinus krefftii*. I am a mammal and a marsupial. I live with about 64 other Northern Hairy-nosed Wombats in a colony of burrows in Epping Forest National Park (Scientific), north-west of Clermont in central Queensland. Ours is the only colony left in the world. We are a critically endangered species.

Nº 4

Male 25

Lasiorhinus krefftii

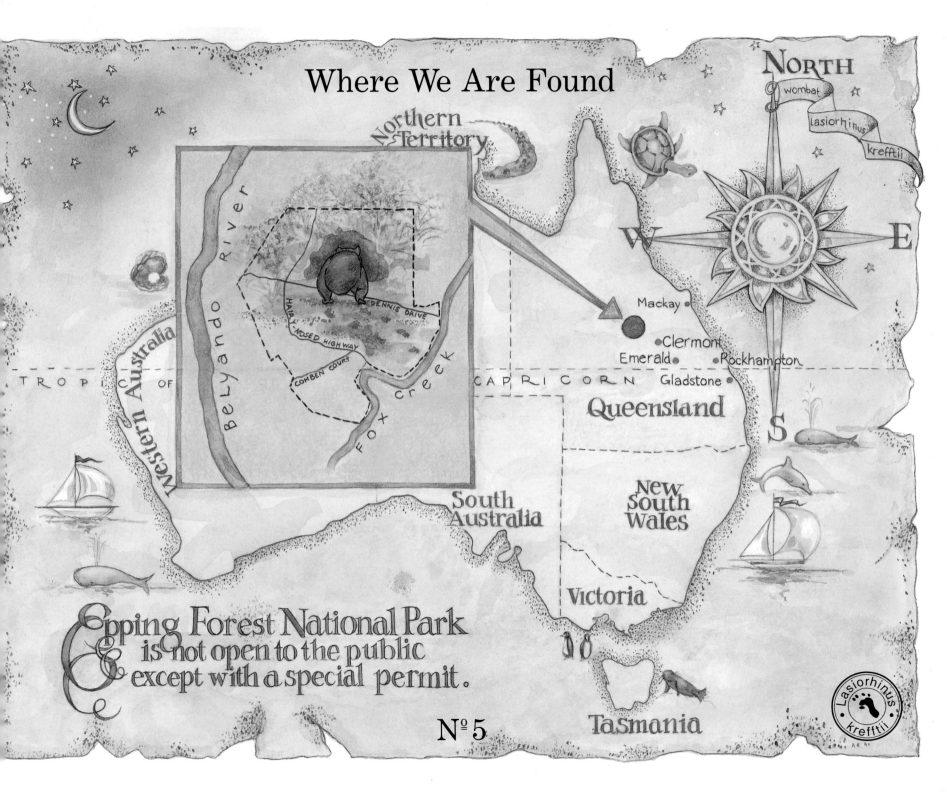

Where We Are Found

Our Pre-historic Ancestors

Diprotodons are ancestors of both wombats and koalas. Until about 10 000 years ago they were found all over Australia. There were many species of diprotodons. *Diprotodon optatum*, weighing up to 2 000 kilograms, was about as big as a rhinoceros.

Diprotodons were herbivorous. The female had a pouch.

In South Australia a fossilised diprotodon joey has been found with the mother's skeleton, in the area where her pouch would have been.

Diprotodons had two very long front teeth – like wombats!

The koalas took to the trees and we wombats stayed on the ground.

A Giant Wombat species *Phascolonus gigas* was found in Australia until about 100 000 years ago. It was herbivorous and carried its young in a pouch.

Possums, kangaroos, koalas and wombats all belong to the Order Diprotodonta.

The skull of a Giant Wombat has been found at the Wellington Caves in New South Wales. Wombat fossils have been found in Western Australia; and fossils of a Pygmy Wombat have been found in Victoria.

modern wombat

Lasiorhinus kreffftii

Modern Wombats

Wombats are mammals and also marsupials.

Wombats are fossorial herbivores.

Wombats have long front teeth for chewing.

Their teeth keep growing all their lives.

strong sense of smell

tough, thick-skinned hide

front leg with five fingers

back leg with four toes and a lumpy 'half toe'

diet: mostly grass

square cube-shaped droppings

small tail

sharp claws like chisels for digging

A new-born wombat is as small as a bean. It crawls to the pouch and suckles on a teat for about six months then for another six months shares its time between the pouch and the outside world.

In some parts of Australia, wombats are poisoned with gas released into their burrows. In some parts of Australia, wombats are shot.

Wombats lie on their sides to scratch and scrape at the walls of their tunnels.

Wombats bulldoze the soil away from their burrows by walking backwards.

Wombats are determined excavators, clever engineers and creative architects.

Lasiorhinus krefftii

Telling Wombat Species Apart

Common Wombats and Southern Hairy-nosed Wombats are not endangered species, although in some areas human progress is shrinking their habitat.

Northern Hairy-nosed Wombat

Lasiorhinus krefftii

long, pointed ears

very wide face, very flat hairy snout

black patches around eyes

silky fur

grey with brown flecks

Southern Hairy-nosed Wombat

Lasiorhinus latifrons

long, pointed ears

wide face, flat hairy snout

silky fur

dark grey/dark brown

Common Wombat

Vombatus ursinus

short, rounded ears

pointed face, bare snout

tough fur

black/grey/light brown /gold

Lasiorhinus krefftii

Where We Used to be Found

Northern Hairy-nosed Wombats were not always found only in the north. They were once found across a large area including northern Victoria, New South Wales and Queensland.

Since the time of the first European settlement, specimens of Northern Hairy-nosed Wombats have been collected from three areas: Deniliquin, the Moonie River near St George, and Clermont.

The present colony at Epping Forest used to extend further north to Mount Coolon, west of Mackay. In the past people reported seeing Northern Hairy-nosed Wombats at Mount Douglas and Highland Plain, Injune, Tambo, Baralaba, on the Alice River, in the Balonne-Maranoa river system and in Carnarvon National Park.

unconfirmed sightings

present colony

confirmed sightings

Naming a Wombat

Lasiorhinus means 'hairy rhinarium (nose)'; *krefftii* is in honour of Johann Krefft, Australia's first mammal palaeontologist.

Our species was not always called *Lasiorhinus krefftii*.

In 1872 a wombat fossil was found in the Wellington Caves, New South Wales. It was named *krefftii*. The species it came from was thought to be extinct.

In 1900 wombat skulls were sent to the Queensland Museum by Mr Gillespie of St George in south-western Queensland. They were given the name *Phascolomys gillespiei*.

In 1937 wombat skins were sent from Clermont in central Queensland to the Queensland Museum by the Barnard brothers. It was thought that the skins came from a sub-species of the Southern Hairy-nosed Wombat *Lasiorhinus latifrons*, so they were called *Lasiorhinus latifrons barnardi*.

In 1983 scientists realised the fossil, the skulls and the skins all belonged to the same species. So we were called *Lasiorhinus krefftii* (Northern Hairy-nosed Wombat).

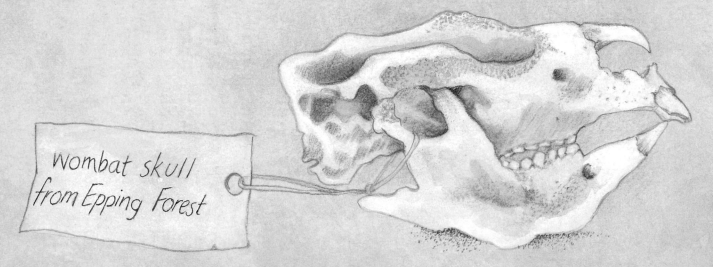

Wombat skull from Epping Forest

Lasiorhinus krefftii

The Wombat Seekers

In 1937, two brothers called Charles (Chas) and Greensill (H.G.) Barnard of Duaringa outside Rockhampton were commissioned by the Queensland Museum to investigate a 'new kind of wombat' in the Clermont District. They shot one of the wombats and sent the skin to the museum.

In letters to the museum, they said they were mystified about what the 'Queensland wombats' ate. They didn't even know if we ate underground or above the ground. They had a hard time catching us, because we're nocturnal, we're fast runners and we have lots of burrows to hide in.

The Barnards followed up rumours of wombats at Tambo, Aramac, Jericho, Blackall and on the Alice River but didn't find any more colonies. They began to realise how precious we are.

Coomooboolaroo
Duaringa
Oct 2nd 1937

My brother and I returned yesterday from another Wombat hunt. After a round trip of nearly 800 miles I regret I have to say that we were unsuccessful in obtaining any more specimens of Wombat. We spent a whole week at the place where we secured the first one &, although we kept going night and day, & having traps out, we did not see even one & had to come to the conclusion that there were very few animals in the area. There might be one hundred burrows in a distance of two miles by half-mile, but from the tracks there might be only twenty animals...If they are as scarce as they seem to be, it was good luck to secure the one we got, as it may not be long before they are extinct...

With kind regards
Yours sincerely
Chas Barnard

Coomooboolaroo
Duaringa
June 11th 1939

My brother H.G. joins me in thanking you for sending us the description of the Clermont Wombat and are rather proud that our name has been tacked onto what may shortly become an extinct animal.

With kind regards
Yours sincerely
Chas Barnard

jasmine flowers

Wild orange flowers bloom at midnight.

There used to be a range of native grasses at Epping Forest. Buffel grass was introduced for cattle and is now taking over. We are being forced to eat more and more of this.

Preying Mantis's egg case

Our Home: Flora

corkscrew grass

Epping Forest National Park covers about 3 000 hectares. Our colony has burrows on about 300 hectares. The burrows are in groups, with tracks between them. Mostly only one wombat lives in each burrow but we are always digging new burrows and renovating old ones. One burrow might have several entrances. Some of our tunnels are four metres deep and 30 metres long.

Our home is in the soft, orange-coloured sandy soil of an old watercourse, which supports trees, shrubs, grasses and sedges.

seeds like the rotor blade of a helicopter

buffel grass

Tough but fragile native grasses – ready to fly, whizz and spin!

Pink star flowers in spring attract a host of butterflies.

Caper White Butterfly

sedge

Orchids grow on logs and trees.

Lasiorhinus krefftii

Our Home: Fauna

pardalote

Blue-faced Honeyeater

Wedge-tailed Eagle

We share our home with many other mammals, birds, insects, reptiles and frogs. The land is alive with movement, both day and night.

Pardalotes build their nests in the bank above our burrows.

Rufous Bettong

wombat

Sand Goanna

Dingo

Pied Butcherbird

Sulphur-crested Cockatoo

Spotted Bowerbird
(gathers white objects)

Eastern Grey Kangaroo

By day ants carry seedheads of buffel grass into their subterranean tunnels. By night tiny reptiles bob up from holes hidden under plants.

Caper White Butterfly

Holy Cross Frog

These sketches are not to scale.

gecko

Lasiorhinus krefftii

Changes to Our Habitat

Cattle came to central Queensland in the 1860s –
There were more wombats then.
Heavy hooves sank into the sandy soil,
Caused avalanches at our entrances.
Heavy bodies collapsed our burrows.
Heavy hides rested in the shade of trees
Whose roots supported our tunnels.
Cattle competed with us for grass –
The cattle also chewed on leaves
but we
Weren't tall enough for trees.

In 1971 Epping Forest was declared a National Park.
The cattle and horses were removed in 1981.

Some people didn't like their working animals
Falling down holes.
Some people shot my family.
Some – desperate in drought – couldn't afford to care
But noticed when we were gone.
People brought weeds, foxes, rabbits, cats –
If only the land had stayed the same!
And now there are only about 65 of us –
No relatives anywhere –
The Northern Hairy-noses are almost gone.
Now everyone cares.

A female Northern Hairy-nosed Wombat called Joan lived
in captivity for 27 years with a family in central Queensland.

N° 17

Humans

These humans are funny!
They dig in the heat.
They gather our droppings –
Is that what they eat?

They have two sets of fingers
And tracks with no toes!
I can smell when they're near
With my big hairy nose.

They have two eyes for daytime
And three for the night.
I can see in the dark –
They seem to need light.

But when I come out
From my home underground,
And their silver trap shuts
With a frightening sound,

I know that these humans
Will look after me;
Just study me gently
And then set me free.

Male 25

PS I've been trapped 58 times.
Most of my friends
have been trapped
once or twice.

Dr Alan Horsup

Bauhinia leaves look like butterflies against the sky.

1 – 50   ♂
51 – 100 ♀
101 –   ♂

Male 25
33kg

№ 19

Lasiorhinus krefftii

A Helping Hand

walk-through trap

Once everyone realised the danger we were in, scientists in many different fields started studying us: ecologists, zoologists, botanists, biologists, pathologists, palaeontologists, geneticists and theriologists.

They counted our burrows and entrances. They studied how often we came out of our burrows to eat. They studied our metabolism. They compared us with other wombats.

computerised radio collar

Nº 20

They made special traps to catch us at the entrances to our burrows without disturbing us too much. They tattooed numbers into our ears. They implanted microchips under our skin so we could be identified by scanner.

They developed computerised collars which measured movement, temperature and light, to find out how long we ate; how long we slept; at what temperature we left our burrows; how long we stayed in the dark and how long we spent in the light of the stars.

They studied our droppings to see which parasites were in our stomachs. They studied the droppings of other animals to see if they had been eating us. They studied the grasses we eat.

They set up fire control measures. They put out supplementary food for us – but we didn't bother with it much.

They set hair traps with double-sided sticky tape at the entrance to our burrows to record the DNA of each animal.

They wrote a Wombat Recovery Plan and set up a Wombat Recovery Team of scientists, rangers, park neighbours and helpers from all over Australia.

PS I once went to the vet in Clermont when I had an injured leg.

radio collar

Lasiorhinus krefftii

Eastern Barred Bandicoots in Victoria, Brush-tailed Bettongs in South Australia and Western Swamp Tortoises in Western Australia have been saved from extinction by removing a few individuals to a captive breeding colony to produce offspring for future release.

The captive breeding program for Northern Hairy-nosed Wombats began on 22 June 1996.

N⁰ 22

The Wombat
Who Talked to the Stars

There was only a small circlet of moon on the night
Male 104 left the eastern entrance to Burrow 5,
heading for his favourite feeding ground.

Nº 23

104, a young male of about two years and weighing 22 kilograms, was mature and strong, with silky fur and supple skin. After six months in his mother's pouch, and weaning at about 12 months, he was now used to living on his own.

There had been rain in the past few weeks, and the tussocks around Burrow 5 were producing tasty green shoots. Without walking very far or using much energy, 104 could have a good feed, a little sit on the sandy soil and a little talk to the stars, and be back in the burrow before morning.

Tonight he had chosen to come up through the eastern entrance to his burrow. But all three entrances had been covered with large silver traps.

104's tiny feet tracked gently over the sand hiding the bars of the trap and the black rubber matting underneath. His padded toes just missed the trip-wire of fishing-line which had been set to snap a rat trap above his head. The snapping of the rat trap would make the doors of the wombat trap drop shut – and send a radio signal back to camp.

Although there were females about, there was nothing on 104's mind but food. He was not yet concerned with finding a mate.

He had a little sit on the ground outside his burrow, and looked around at the stars. The Southern Cross was showing clearly above its pointers and Jupiter was shining brightly in the western sky.

104 padded off to have a nibble on a tussock he had enjoyed the night before. He left some droppings on the path to a neighbouring burrow and rubbed his bottom against his favourite tree, a small shrub with rough bark and tiny leaves. Sandy soil from his fur clung to the bark and a fine powdering of soil sifted over the ground.

Dawn was lighting the sky. Time to go home. The silver contraption at the entrance to the burrow had caused no trouble on the way out. Why would it be a problem now?

One padded foot hit the trip-wire of fishing-line. The rat trap snapped shut. Two steel doors dropped. A signal was sent back to base camp. Something had set off the alarm at Trap 12 above Burrow 5.

When the people arrived and walked to the trap quietly so as not to upset their captive, 104 was standing still, head down, hoping to move forward and go down into his tunnel.

Nº 27

But this was no ordinary trapping. The scientists had been looking for a young male to send on a special mission. I would have liked to be chosen – but I was too old.

104 was kept in a quiet, dark and cool place until his plane arrived. Then he flew off to a zoo, to a future full of loving care and any food he cared to eat.

'What name shall we give you?' wondered the scientists. 'We can't keep calling you 104!'

Then Peter (one of the scientists) realised the date. It was the 22nd of June! The winter solstice.

I'm sure 'Solstice' will do us proud, starting a new colony somewhere else. It's a bit like a human going off to form a settlement on a new planet. When a female joins him, they'll send their joeys back home.

Does anyone need an old wombat who'd like to fly?

We don't know if wombats talk to stars. We know they talk to one another. And from tracks and observations we know that they sometimes come out of their burrows, sit upright on their bottoms and look around at the night.

Early in the morning of 22 June 1996 (the winter solstice), 'Solstice' was flown to the Western Plains Zoo in Dubbo to begin a captive breeding colony.

Jill Morris

Acknowledgement of Sources
& Reading References

Crossman, Doug. *Population Ecology and Diet of the Northern Hairy-nosed Wombat, Lasiorhinus krefftii (Owen)* Research Report to World Wildlife Fund for Project 64, Queensland National Parks and Wildlife Service, Rockhampton, 1988

Flannery, Tim *The Future Eaters: An ecological history of the Australian lands and people*, Reed, 1994

Horsup, Alan *The Northern Hairy-nosed Wombat Recovery Program: Trials and Triumphs* (in press) Proceedings of the Back from the Brink Conference (Australian Nature Conservation Agency), Sydney, 1995

Johnson, Chris. *Behaviour & Ecology of the Northern Hairy-nosed Wombat, Lasiorhinus krefftii (Report to Queensland National Parks and Wildlife Service)*, 1991

Morris, Jill, illus. Burrell, Jane *Golden Wombats*, Harcourt Brace Jovanovich, Sydney, 1990

Morris, Jill, illus. Richardson, Rich *Harry the Hairy-nosed Wombat*, Lloyd O'Neil, Melbourne, 1970

Murray, Peter *Australia's Prehistoric Animals*, Methuen, 1984

Pearson, Steve & Alison *Plants of Central Queensland*, The Society for Growing Australian Native Plants, 1989

Queensland National Parks and Wildlife Service *Recovery Plan for the Northern Hairy-nosed Wombat*, 1991

Schouten, Peter, Quirk, Susan & Archer, Michael (eds) *Prehistoric Animals of Australia*, Australian Museum, 1983

Strahan, Ronald (ed) *The Mammals of Australia*, Australian Museum/Reed Books, Sydney, 1995

Triggs, Barbara *The Wombat: Common Wombats in Australia*, University of New South Wales Press, Sydney, 1995

Triggs, Barbara *Tracks, Scats and other Traces - A Field Guide to Australian Mammals*, Oxford University Press, 1996

Thanks to the Collection: John Oxley Library for permission to use photographs for reference for pages 16 & 17.

Thanks to the Queensland Museum for permission to quote from the Barnard Letters (1937–39).

Glossary

arc — curve

biologist — scientist who studies the life of animals or plants

botanist — scientist who studies plant life

captive breeding colony — colony of animals set up in a safe environment to increase breeding of the species for future release of the young

commissioned — contracted for payment

critically endangered — 'facing an extremely high risk of extinction in the wild in the immediate future'

diprotodon — pre-historic mammal: its name means two front teeth

DNA — Deoxyribonucleic acid: the main carrier of genetic information about a living organism

ecologist — scientist who studies the relation between organisms and environment

elliptic — arc

extinct — (species) no longer in existence

fauna — animal life

flora — plant life

fossil — remains of plant or animal from an earlier era buried in the earth

fossorial — burrowing

geneticist — scientist who studies genes and reproduction in people or animals

habitat — environment inhabited by an animal

herbivorous — eating plants

Lasiorhinus krefftii — (scientific name : lasios=hairy; rhis=nose; krefftii=named after Krefft)

Lasiorhinus latifrons — 'broad-headed hairy-nose'

mammals — animals which are haired and produce milk for their young

marsupial — mammal with a pouch

metabolism — balance between intake of food and water and use of energy

microchip — small chip for storing electronic data

nocturnal — moving about mostly at night

Order — classification of animals to show related groups

pathologist — scientist who studies diseases

palaeontologist — scientist who studies fossils of animals

parasites — animal life living on or inside another (host) animal

Phascolonus gigas — from Greek phaskolos= pouch; gigas=giant

reproduction — production of young

sedges — different from grasses: they are usually triangular in cross-section and are often associated with wet areas

solstice — when the sun in its elliptic is at its furthest point from the Equator (winter/summer)

supple — with ease of movement

theriologist — scientist who studies mammals

Vombatus ursinus — 'bear-like wombat'

wombat — from an Aboriginal word reported by Matthew Flinders to Governor Hunter, and sounding like 'wombach'

zoologist — scientist who studies animal life

Index